happiness is …
快樂就是……

happiness is ...

500 things to be happy about

快樂就是……
500個生活裡的小幸福

麗莎・史瓦琳 & 拉夫・羅拉薩
Lisa Swerling & Ralph Lazar

遠流出版公司

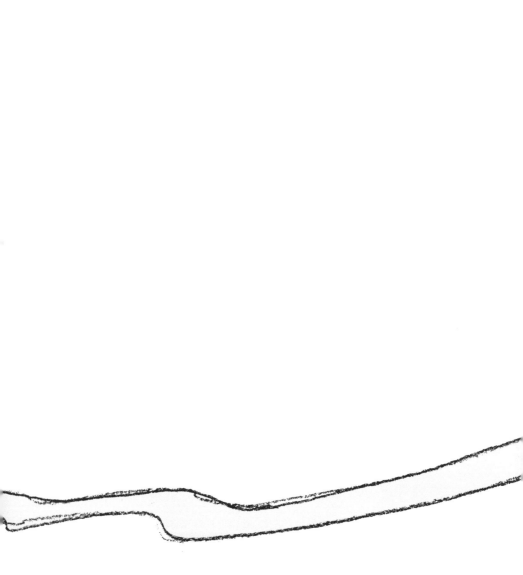

the start of a journey
旅途的起點

a pinky promise
打勾勾

the chocolate bar you
forgot you had
找到先前買了忘記吃
的巧克力棒

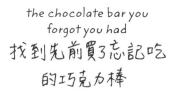

when the vending
machine gives you extra
自動販賣機的商品
多掉出了一份

a view of rooftops
綿延無盡的屋頂

spooning
相擁而眠

pottery on the wheel
動手做手拉坯

extra pepperoni
加料的辣香腸披薩

when a ladybug
lands on you
一隻小瓢蟲停在你身上

a picnic
去野餐

hitting a piñata

玩派對遊戲皮納塔

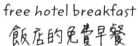

free hotel breakfast
飯店的免費早餐

talking music with
someone who gets it
跟內行人聊音樂

growing a good beard
留一把帥氣的鬍子

simplicity

單純就好

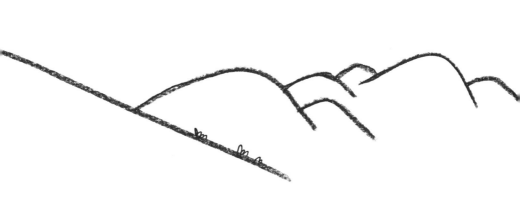

school friends
在學校交到朋友

falling asleep to the sound
of your cat purring
貓咪呼嚕聲伴你入眠

piggyback rides
有人揹你

a rocking chair
坐搖椅

an unexpected upgrade
to business class
意外升級成商務艙

15

*joining a line
just before it
gets really long*
剛好趕在隊伍變長
之前排到隊

*bumping into an
old teacher*
遇到之前的老師

a pancake
breakfast

吃煎餅當早餐

when you're really excited to
show something to someone

急著把某樣東西和某個人分享

tropical drinks

清涼消暑熱帶風味飲

music that takes
you back

音樂勾起美好回憶,

blowing out birthday candles

吹熄生日蠟燭

dancing like idiots
瘋瘋癲癲地跳舞

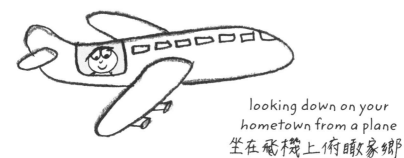

looking down on your
hometown from a plane
坐在飛機上俯瞰家鄉

being the first one up
早上第一個醒來

no dirty dishes in the sink
水槽裡沒有碗要洗

a freshly sharpened
pencil
削得尖尖的鉛筆

finding the perfect
pair of glasses
找到最適合你的眼鏡

spinning on an
office chair
坐在辦公椅上轉啊轉

having your work appreciated
工作表現被稱讚了

saying the same thing at the same time
兩個人異口同聲

doggy breath
跟狗狗親親

finding coins in the sofa
在沙發縫裡找到零錢

24

waking up to a beautiful day

睡醒時陽光正明媚

chasing fireflies
追螢火蟲

when someone's laugh is
funnier than the joke

有人笑得比笑話本身還誇張

being unapologetically
yourself

勇敢做自己

fancy stinky cheese
享用臭臭的高級乳酪

skiing
滑雪

using a pen 'til the very last drop of ink

把一枝筆寫到墨水耗盡

having weird friends

擁有一些特立獨行的朋友

a long bath with a
good book
一邊悠閒泡澡，
一邊讀本好書

breakfast in bed
在床上吃早餐

a hug
擁抱

a spoonful of
peanut butter
挖一大匙花生醬

fixing
something
把東西修好

kids helping without being asked
小孩自動自發做家事

33

sunrise from a surfboard
衝浪看日出

ocking out in the car with
the windows down

搖下車窗，跟著音樂
動ち動ち

passing notes during lectures
上課傳紙條

laughing at a bad movie
被爛電影逗樂

secretly holding hands
偷偷地牽手

meeting someone who loves the
same books you do
遇到閱讀品味相同的人

peeling a tangerine
in one piece
把橘子皮完完整整地剝下來

new guitar strings
吉他換上新弦

a library

圖書館

when you look fabulous
in a group photo

在團體照裡
看起來超上相

when someone else
catches the spider
for you
有人幫你打蜘蛛

going really high on a swing

鞦韆盪得高高的

a warm cat curled up
on your lap

一隻貓咪蜷在你腿上，暖暖的

sugar cubes

方糖

silly mirrors

哈哈鏡

finding a lid that fits
your Tupperware
找到一個大小
剛好的蓋子

stopping to smell the flowers
停下來聞聞花香

a sleeping baby
小嬰兒睡著了

teaching
教學

maple syrup on vanilla
ice cream
楓糖淋上香草冰淇淋

twinkle lights
一閃一閃小燈泡

making a
baby laugh
逗寶寶笑

building a treehouse

蓋樹屋

making a list of all the places
you want to visit
把想去的地方列成一張清單

being forgiven
做錯事被原諒

a wood-burning stove
燒木柴的暖爐

identifying constellations

辨認星座

finding the keys
找到鑰匙

yoga
練瑜珈

cuddles
窩在一起

watching children
play make-believe
看小孩玩扮家家酒

Bubble Wrap
捏氣泡袋

a new language
學習新語言

making a wish and
believing it will come true
許願，相信願望會成真

free mini bottles of
shampoo at a hotel

飯店送的免費洗髮精小瓶子

talking to your
mom when
you're sad

難過的時候
跟媽媽聊聊

shopping

血拼

an adventure
with a camera
帶相機去冒險

standing up for a cause
為公義挺身而出

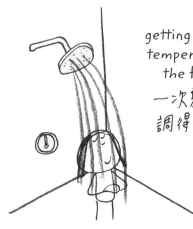

getting the shower
temperature right
the first time
一次就把水溫
調得剛剛好

a ceiling fan
天花板有電風扇

a tax credit
收到退稅

when each sock has a pair
襪子都成雙成對

fresh snow and a sled
剛下過雪，而且有雪橇

falling in love
墜入愛河

waking up and realizing you
don't have to go in to work
醒來時想到今天不用上班

twirling your hair
用手指捲頭髮

being annoying
on purpose
故意鬧別人

the freedom of travel
旅行的自由

staying in on a Friday night
星期五晚上待在家

a child saying "thank you"
without being prompted
小孩主動說謝謝，
不用人催

picking berries
on a sunny day
星期天去採野莓

calling in sick
請病假

the first step
寶寶走出第一步

an Aha! moment
靈光乍現的瞬間

fireworks

看煙火

blowing bubbles
吹泡泡

watching a kid eat an ice-cream cone

看小孩吃甜筒冰淇淋

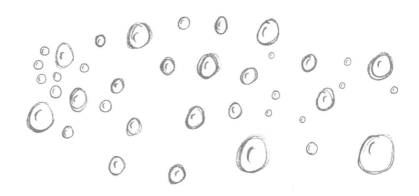

waking up next to the
love of your life
在一生摯愛的身旁醒來

a bowl of perfectly ripe
strawberries
一盒熟透的草莓

eating last night's pizza
for breakfast
把昨晚剩下的披薩當早餐

drinking wine in good company
和好朋友飲酒同樂

sewing by hand
親手縫紉

having a best friend
擁有最要好的朋友

pool noodles
玩塑膠管

scissors sliding through
wrapping paper
用剪刀剪開包裝紙的感覺

a window seat on a bus
坐公車時坐在窗邊

messing around on a boat

坐船四處晃蕩

taking goofy pictures
拍鬼臉照

a front-door good-night kiss
在門口吻別

watching waves crashing

看著海浪滾滾

bacon
培根

the sight of the
pizza-delivery
guy
看到披薩外送員來了

winning a board game
玩桌遊贏了

getting to the
bar just in time
for happy hour
趕上酒吧的
優惠時段

a day spent in nature
用一整天享受大自然

playing with cousins
跟親戚一起玩

an unexpected discount
at checkout
結帳時發現有打折

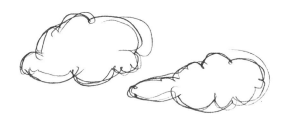

the wind just before a
summer storm
夏日暴雨前的風

getting lost
in a beautiful
painting
沉醉在一幅
美麗的畫中

finding money in
jeans you haven't
worn in a while
在好久沒穿的
褲子口袋裡找到錢

seeing a cheerful umbrella
看見一頂顏色鮮豔的雨傘

celebrating with a little bubbly
喝氣泡酒慶祝

chocolate chip cookies fresh from the oven
熱騰騰剛出爐的巧克力餅乾

discovering a great new song
發現一首好聽的新歌

pretending to be a mermaid
in a swimming pool
在泳池假裝自己是美人魚

finding a power outlet at the airport

在機場找到插座

recovering data from a
dead computer
從當掉的電腦順利
把資料搶救回來

holding a baby chick
抓起一隻小雞

hearing your parents'
stories from back in
the day
聽爸媽講他們
年輕時的往事

a high school reunion
參加高中同學會

sitting beneath a willow tree
坐在柳樹下

rolling down all the
windows and letting
your hair fly

把全部車窗都搖下來，
讓頭髮迎風飛舞

貴賓通道

not having to wait in line
不需要排隊等候

a duet
四手聯彈

the cold side of
the pillow
枕頭還沒
被睡熱的那一側

watching a friend get married
參加朋友的婚禮

jumping into a lake
跳進湖裡

making lists

列清單

having the elevator already
waiting on your floor

不用等電梯

video games
玩電動

buying flowers
for yourself
買花給自己

building a
snowman
堆雪人

an ambitious moustache
留一把狂放的鬍子

a photo booth
去拍快照

dancing the tango
跳探戈

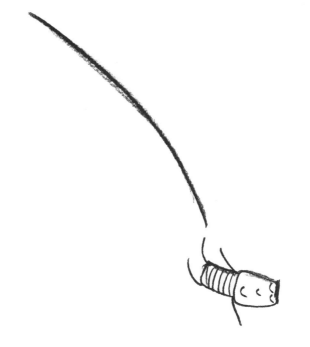

knowing that there is someone
there to catch you

知道有人會接住你

autumn leaves
秋日落葉

a fully charged cell phone

手機電池充得飽飽的

running through
sprinklers

在灑水器上
跑來跑去

making s'mores

做綿花糖夾心餅乾

having a partner
in crime
有人陪你當共犯

a big hug from a
small person
身材小小的人給你
大大的擁抱

when the dish you
ordered turns out to be
the best at the table
你點的餐是整桌裡面
最好吃的

meditating
靜心

being winked at by
someone nice

有個條件不錯的人對
你眨了眨眼

riding bicycles

騎著腳踏車

looking forward, not back
往前看，而不是倒退

a mother's cooking

媽媽的家常菜

finally peeing when you
really need to

忍了一陣子，
尿急終於解放

riding in a car parallel to a fast-moving train

開著車，和一列高速行進的火車並肩疾駛

when your favorite sushi comes around on the conveyor belt

吃迴轉壽司時，最愛的壽司剛好轉到面前

people-watching
觀察行人

a comfortable silence
自在的沉默

remembering that word you
couldn't remember yesterday
記起你昨天一直想不起來的那個字

feeling you are
heading in the
right direction
感覺到你走的
方向是對的

writing on a
steamy mirror
在起霧的鏡子上寫字

snorting while laughing
笑的時候不小心發出豬叫聲

using chopsticks
correctly

正確使用筷子

getting lost in a novel
沉迷於小說裡

changing your own tire

自己換輪胎

cheese

乳酪

an empty inbox

收信匣空蕩蕩

sunshine through the leaves

陽光從樹葉間灑落

being home alone

一個人在家

cotton candy
棉花糖

going through old photos
回顧舊照片

being your own boss
自己當家做主

feeling safe in
someone's arms
在某人懷抱中
感到安心

laughing so hard that milk
comes out of your nose
笑到牛奶從鼻孔噴出來

the sound of popcorn popping

爆米花爆開的聲音

new plants

新盆栽

the view of clouds from a plane

從飛機上望出去的雲海

finally
getting that
mosquito

總算打死
那隻蚊子

sock skating around
the house

穿襪子在家裡溜冰

remembering something totally hilarious
in a silent situation

在安靜的地方，突然想到超爆笑的事情

doing nothing all day long
耍廢一整天

a coworker who becomes a friend

跟同事變成好友

reading trashy
novels without guilt

理直氣壯地看沒營養的小說

freckles

有雀斑

walking a dog (or two)
帶隻狗出門散步（或帶兩隻）

receiving unexpected mail
意料之外的來信

a compliment
from a stranger
陌生人的讚美

housemates
becoming a family
跟室友變得像家人

being brave
勇往直前

when you feel a bite on the line

感覺到有魚上鉤了

trying something new
嘗試新事物

when you love
your job
熱愛你的工作

seeing your breath
in cold air

天氣冷時，
呼出白白的熱氣

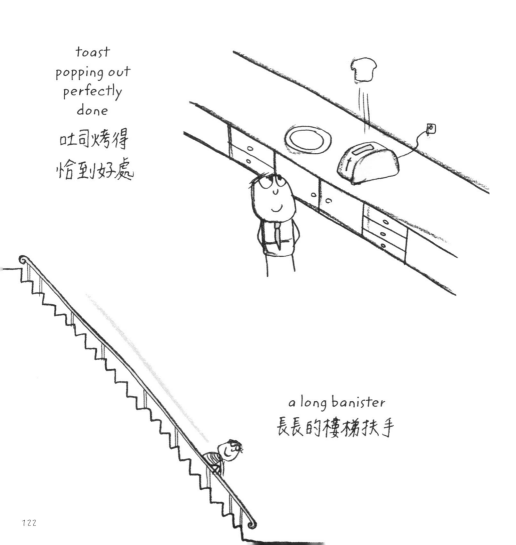

toast
popping out
perfectly
done

吐司烤得
恰到好處

a long banister

長長的樓梯扶手

erasing the
whiteboard

把白板擦乾淨

putting on a
wetsuit

穿上潛水衣

traveling without kids

出門玩不必帶著拖油瓶

platitudes that actually
make you feel better
有些話雖然很老套，
但確實讓你心情比較好一點

一切都會好的

a sleepover
住朋友家

looking up at the world from
under water

從水底看世界

hunkering down in a cozy coffee shop

在一間舒適的咖啡館裡窩著

when
someone
stands up
for you
有人為你發聲

napping
outdoors
在室外睡午覺

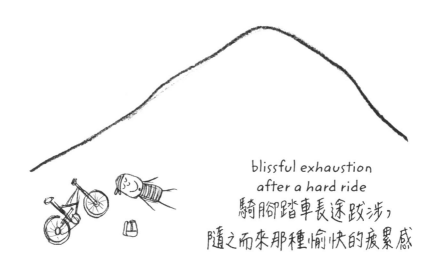

blissful exhaustion
after a hard ride
騎腳踏車長途跋涉,
隨之而來那種愉快的疲累感

coming home to your dog
回到家有愛犬迎接

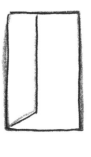

falling asleep in the room you grew up in
睡在從小用到大的房間裡

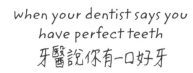

when your dentist says you
have perfect teeth
牙醫說你有一口好牙

making it to the gas station on "E"
汽油用光時剛好趕到加油站

not taking yourself
too seriously

不要太苛求自己

finding the last pair
of clean socks

找到最後一雙乾淨襪子

when you tear a page from
a notebook and its edge is
perfectly neat

從筆記本上整整齊齊撕下一頁

making that shot into the
wastepaper basket

把紙球精準地投進了廢紙簍

crêpes!

可麗餅！

a view of the sea

眼前一片海景

an unexpected
bouquet

意外收到一束花

remembering that you still have coffee in your cup

想起杯子裡還有咖啡

kids eating their food without complaint

小孩乖乖吃完飯，不嫌東嫌西

warm clothes straight
out of the dryer

剛烘乾的衣服暖呼呼

a long massage

做一次長長的按摩

when your favorite song
comes on to the radio
廣播剛好放到你的愛歌

knowing you're
both a little crazy
知道你身邊也有個
瘋瘋顛顛的人

a well-dressed dog
穿漂亮衣服的狗狗

your boss taking the day off
主管請假

no homework
沒有作業

*your favorite team winning
at the last minute*

你支持的球隊在最後關頭逆轉勝

knowing where
you belong
屬於某個團體

bubblegum
吹泡泡糖

first tracks on fresh snow
剛下過雪，雪地上第一道足跡

doing something
stupid and laughing
about it for weeks

做了一件蠢事，
為此笑了好幾個星期

when you're angry
with someone and they
make you laugh

你在生某人的氣，
但他卻逗你笑了

beating your own record
打破自己的紀錄

when you suddenly
understand the
meaning of a song
突然理解某首歌的意境

bedtime stories
睡前故事

when the bus arrives just as you arrive
剛到站牌的時候，公車也剛好來了

checking in at the airport
for a vacation
辦登機手續準備去度假

coming home to dinner on the table
回到家,桌上就有準備好的晚餐

wearing clothes that make
you feel beautiful
穿漂漂亮亮的衣服

a good high five
擊掌

handwritten letters
親筆寫信

the view from a ski lift
從雪場纜車往下眺望的美景

leaving the car wash

車子洗得亮晶晶

laughing so hard you
pee a little

笑到漏尿

watching the
clock hit 5:00

看著時針指向5點

eye contact
with someone
you fancy

和你欣賞的人對上眼

already having all the ingredients
for a recipe

食譜上的材料家裡都有

talented
street performers
有才華的街頭藝術家

rolling down a grassy hill
滾下草坡

148

untamable
curly hair
野性美波浪捲

a fresh lemon
新鮮的檸檬

wearing a tutu
穿芭蕾舞衣

finally
getting the
Hula-Hoop
going
總算讓
拉圈轉起來

149

salty pistachios
鹽味開心果

being rescued when
you're locked out
忘記帶鑰匙的時候
有人來救你

self-confidence
有自信

watching the trailers,
looking forward to the movie
一邊看電影開始前的預告，
一邊期待本片開始

recharging

充電

opening a book
you read on
holiday and
beach sand
falls out

打開假日看的書，
掉出海灘沙

peeling the protective
sticker off a new
gadget

撕掉新產品上的
保護膜

homegrown produce
自己種菜

balloon animals
動物氣球

fitting everything in
your suitcase
順利把所有東西收進行李箱

olives
橄欖

receiving the first
birthday call just
as the clock strikes
midnight

零時一到，就收到
第一通生日祝賀電話

a convertible
開敞篷車兜風

being together
有人相伴

yelling from the top
of a mountain and
hearing your echo

站在山頂大叫，
聽見自己的回音

a night out with the girls
女孩專屬狂歡夜

the perfect snowball
圓得恰到好處的雪球

daydreaming
做白日夢

when your mom says
your hair looks nice
媽媽誇你的髮型很好看

a water fight
打水仗

decorating cupcakes
裝飾杯子蛋糕

a full tank of gas
油箱加滿

big mountains

高山峻嶺

the sun on
your face on
a cold day
冷天裡有陽光
照在臉上

good health
身體健康

milk & cookies
牛奶配餅乾

an airport reunion

在機場團聚

heading out on a family vacation

全家啟程出遊

a fully stocked kitchen

家裡存糧充足

brand-new running shoes
嶄新的跑鞋

welcoming a baby
into the world
迎接新生命

making art
藝術創作

jumping in a pool
after a long, hot day

忍受漫長又悶熱的一天之後，
跳進泳池

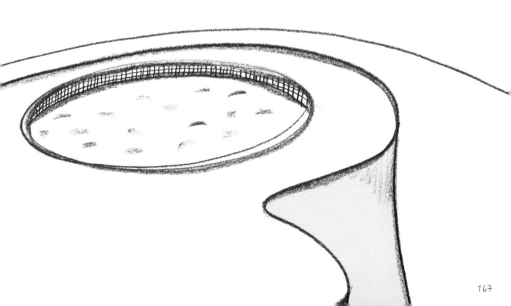

reaching the bottom of
the ironing basket
終於把籃子裡
該燙的衣服都燙完了

doodling
信筆塗鴉

walking down an up escalator
搭手扶梯時往反方向走

gardening
做園藝

warm bread
熱呼呼的麵包

being swung
手拉手轉圈圈

quality time with dad
和爸爸共度美好時光

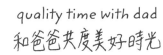

living in your favorite city

住在最愛的城市

dark chocolate
黑巧克力

having choices
擁有選擇

a snow globe
雪花球

glitter!
亮晶晶!

a romantic date

浪漫的約會

finding the perfect
thing to wear
找到最適合
這個場合穿的衣服

a serious
conversation with
a small child
和小孩子進行深度對談

the blissful
scratching of an
itchy bite
抓癢抓到爽

taking a road trip

公路旅行

kissing in the car
在車上接吻

strong coffee
喝杯濃醇咖啡

a new haircut
剪了新髮型

your first paycheck

領到第一份薪水

seeing a plant grow

觀察植物生長

wearing a hat

戴帽子

the smell of rain
下雨天的味道

listening to classical music
聆聽古典音樂

a pillow fight
打枕頭仗

crossing the finish line
抵達終點

margaritas on the
beach
在海灘享受
瑪格麗特調酒

freshly washed towels
剛洗好的毛巾

going to see your
favorite band live
聽最愛的樂團
現場演唱

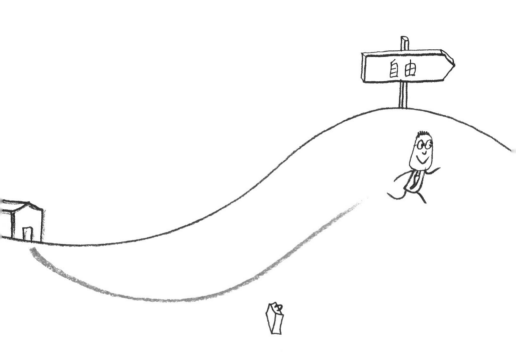

quitting a job you hate
辭掉討厭的工作

a drink of cold water
after a long run

長跑過後喝杯涼水

your favorite pj's

穿最愛的睡衣

the smell of freshly cut grass

草坪剛修剪過的味道

187

summertime
夏日風情

a really sharp
kitchen knife
鋒利的菜刀

a glass of wine in
front of the fire
在火爐前小酌

overhearing the
laughter of your
loved ones
聽見你所愛的人
發出笑聲

air-conditioning on a
hot summer night
炎熱夏夜裡的空調

being on a team
團體合作

cooking with a friend
和朋友一起煮飯

a good hair day
今天頭髮很柔順

getting your old password
right on the first guess

一次就猜到舊密碼

someone putting a blanket
over you while you sleep

有人在你睡著時替你蓋被子

drumming

打鼓

eating chips on the way back from the supermarket

在從超市回家的路上
打開薯片邊走邊吃

sucking up a long piece of spaghetti in a single slurp

「咻」地一下把長長一條
義大利麵吸起來

taking off your boots after a long hike

走了一大段路之後把鞋子脫掉

moving in together and
making a new home

住在一起，建立新家

dining
alfresco

在戶外用餐

finally shaving
after a few days
隔好幾天終於剃了鬍子

finding a new book by
your favorite author
發現最愛的作家出新書

speaking in a
helium voice
用尖尖的聲音講話

a buffet
吃自助餐

texting from under
the blanket

躲在棉被下傳簡訊

the smell of
a baby
小寶寶的味道

not taking yourself
too seriously
放輕鬆過生活

a yo-yo
溜溜球

having a pet rock
養石頭當寵物

knitting
編織

falling asleep to the sound of rain

在雨聲中入睡

jumping over waves
海浪沖過來就跳

karaoke
卡拉OK

bumping into a childhood friend
巧遇童年好友

twins
雙胞胎

a well-made bed
整理好的床鋪

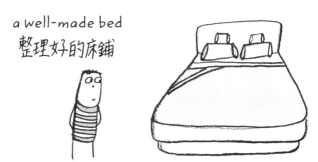

playing in a band

玩樂團

helping a
stranger
隨手助人

crafting things
做手工藝

a hot tub
泡熱水澡

sitting around a
campfire
圍坐在火堆邊

feeling the baby kick
感覺到小寶寶在踢

dancing all night
徹夜跳舞

typing THE END
打下「完結」

the sweet pain after
a hard workout
拼命健身後
令人滿足的痠痛感

hot chocolate
with lots of
whipped cream
熱巧克力上面
擠很多鮮奶油

sunflowers
向日葵

shooting hoops
投籃

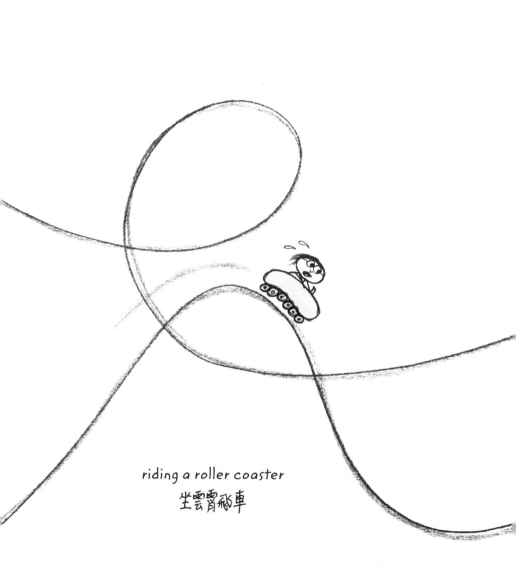

riding a roller coaster

坐雲霄飛車

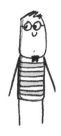

wearing your boyfriend's
oversized T-shirt
穿著男友的上衣

hearing a story about
yourself as a child
聽你小時候的故事

watching cat videos on the Internet
看網路上的貓咪影片

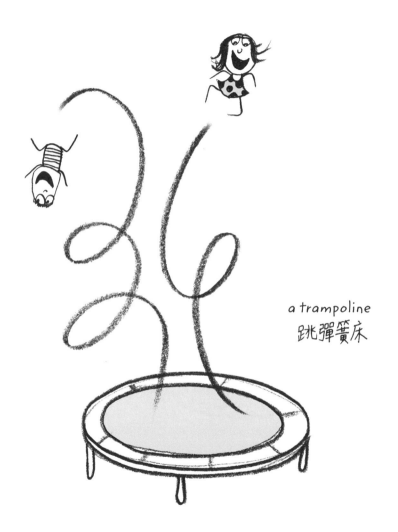

a trampoline

跳彈簧床

cozying up in a dry tent in the rain
下雨時窩在乾爽的帳篷裡

getting rid of extra baggage
拋掉多餘的負擔

a bird landing close
without seeing you
一隻沒注意到你的鳥
停在你附近

choosing flowers in a market
在花店挑花

the afterglow of finishing a novel
讀完小說的餘韻

racing downhill
衝下斜坡

a butterfly
一隻蝴蝶

licking cake batter out of the bowl
把碗裡剩下的麵糊舔光光

laughing 'til your
face aches
笑到臉發疼

strumming
a ukulele
彈奏烏克麗麗

the last second of
your last exam
最後一場考試的
最後一秒

discovering underwater worlds

發掘海底新世界

venting with good friends
跟好朋友抱怨

finally
making a
difficult
decision
終於做出
艱難的抉擇

instant noodles
煮泡麵

kicking a soccer ball
踢足球

eating anything
you want when
you're pregnant
懷孕時想吃什麼就吃什麼

the first page of a
new notebook
新筆記本的第一頁

sharing life with
your soulmate
和靈魂伴侶共度人生

singing in a choir

在合唱團唱歌

a tiny garden
一座小小花園

realizing you love your crazy family, warts and all
領悟到你愛你瘋瘋的家人，即便他們有很多不完美

the smell of early-morning coffee
大清早來杯咖啡

watching clouds change shape
看雲朵變換形狀

cheating on your diet
and losing weight anyway
說好的節食計畫根本沒遵守，
但還是瘦下來了

being a
traveler not
a tourist
當個旅人，
不當觀光客

book club
讀書會

sparklers
玩仙女棒

having dinner
as a family
全家聚在一起吃晚餐

making a giant sandwich
做一份超大的三明治

fresh bagels and cream cheese
新鮮貝果抹奶油乳酪

the mere existence
of the didgeridoo
世上竟然有「迪吉里杜管」
這種樂器

a nice big yawn
用力打個呵欠

making others' lives easier
讓別人的生活輕鬆一些

chatting with grandma

跟奶奶說說話

a bubble bath in
candlelight

燭光泡泡浴

the smell of freshly washed hair
頭髮剛洗好的香味

meeting up with your oldest friend
和老朋友見面

a slinky
翻轉彈簧

uninterrupted TV
看電視不受打擾

the smell of basil
羅勒的香味

finding that perfect shell
找到最漂亮的貝殼

writing when
the words
really flow
寫作靈感源源不絕

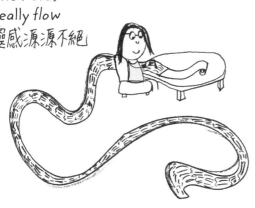

finding a piece of
candy in a bag you
thought was empty

以為袋子空了，
結果找到一顆糖果

noticing it's
11:11 and
making a wish
剛好11:11，
趕快許個願

booking a
vacation
預訂度假行程

watching snowflakes

賞雪

a special pen
一枝特別的筆

pickles
醃黃瓜

unpacking the last box
打開最後一箱行李

an early-morning walk
清晨散步

the fantasy of getting away from it all
幻想遠離塵囂

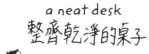

a sneaky weekend break
週末偷偷出去玩

工作　　　海邊
例行公事　放鬆
辦公室　　度假勝地
責任　　　
忙茫茫　　享受人生

watching your man
cook dinner
看你老公準備晚餐

a hot drink on a cold day
冬天喝熱飲

a slice of lime in a
cold bottled beer
在冰啤酒裡加片檸檬

sleeping diagonally
躺對角線睡覺

a great conversation with a stranger
和陌生人聊得很愉快

wearing flowers
in your hair
頭上插幾朵花

reminiscing
話當年

海邊

biking to the beach
騎腳踏車去海邊

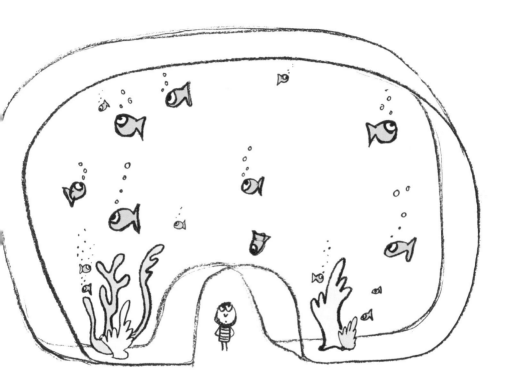

an aquarium

水族館

a long walk with a friend
和朋友悠閒地散步著

setting up your own business
自己創業

hot sauce
辣醬

grandchildren
兒孫滿堂

receiving what you
ordered online
收到網購商品

jumping in puddles
踩積水

resting after a long, hard trek
長途跋涉後的休息

untangling the
last knot
解開最後一個結

when a baby holds your
finger and refuses to let go
小寶寶抓住你的手指不肯放開

steak
牛排

liking
yourself
愛自己

returning to bed
after a long day
經過漫漫長日，上床睡覺

playing in the warm summer rain
溫暖的夏日，在雨中嬉戲

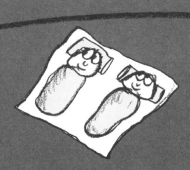

sleeping under the stars
在星夜下睡著

leaving work on Friday
週五下班

being the only one laughing . . .
and not being able to stop
只有你一個人在笑，卻怎麼也停不下來

scaring the living
daylights out of someone
把別人嚇得魂飛魄散

wearing new shoes
for the first time
第一次穿新鞋

being really
silly together
跟朋友一起做傻事

buying yourself
something nice,
just because
替自己買好東西，
不需要什麼理由

a costume party where everyone
makes a huge effort

參加變裝派對，每個人都很用心準備

parenthood
為人父母

pajama parties
睡衣派對

getting your dream job
得到夢寐以求的工作

finding the perfect pair of jeans
找到完美的牛仔褲

being engaged
訂婚

finishing the crossword
解開字謎

a shooting star
有流星

riding a bike downhill

騎腳踏車滑下斜坡

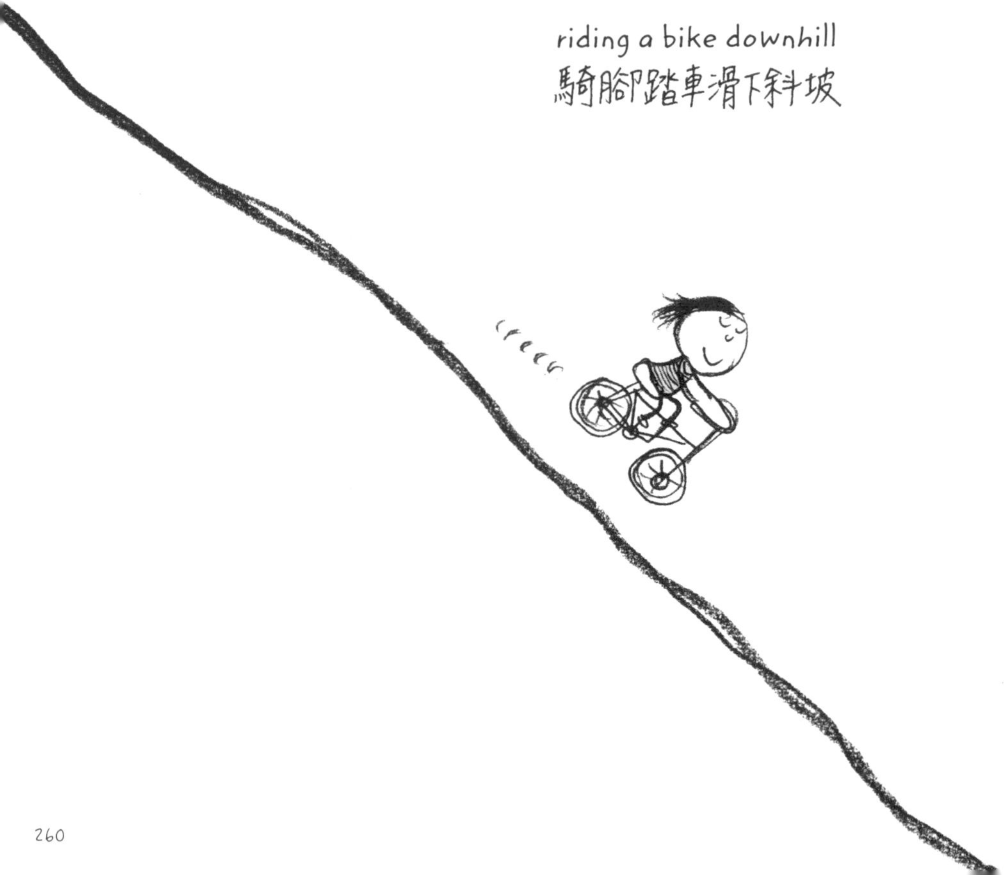

a head massage
頭部按摩

*getting that pesky
piece of food with a
toothpick*
終於用牙籤剔掉
討人厭的菜渣

*dropping your phone and
catching it mid-air*
不小心弄掉手機，
在半空中及時接住

having a dishwasher

有台洗碗機

perfectly painted toes

指甲油塗得完美無瑕

sisterhood

擁有一群好姊妹

free Wi-Fi
免費Wi-Fi

finding your size in
the sale items
在賣場找到自己
可以穿的尺寸

拍賣物品

leaving and never looking back
頭也不回地離開

seeing a stranger smile while
he's reading a book
看見路人邊閱讀邊露出微笑

finishing a
to-do list
解決所有待辦事項

giving a kid a Band-Aid
for a tiny cut
在孩子的小傷口上貼OK繃

receiving a love
letter
收到情書

sharing an umbrella

共撑一把傘

taking off ice skates
脫掉冰刀鞋

roasting marshmallows
烤棉花糖

a fresh baguette
新鮮法式長棍麵包

balloons
氣球

 the first glimpse of home after a long time away
再次看見久別的家鄉

快樂就是…
——500個生活裡的小幸福
Happiness Is . . .
500 Things to Be Happy About

作者	麗莎·史瓦琳 (Lisa Swerling) ＆拉夫·羅拉薩 (Ralph Lazar)
譯者	陳思穎
執行編輯	鄭智妮
行銷企劃	李雙如
內頁排版	張凱揚
封面設計	賴維明
手寫字	石東藏

發行人	王榮文
出版發行	遠流出版事業股份有限公司
地址	臺北市南昌路2段81號6樓
客服電話	02-2392-6899
傳真	02-2392-6658
郵撥	0189456-1
著作權顧問	蕭雄淋律師

2016年11月1日　初版一刷
2018年6月15日　初版九刷
定價　新台幣260元　(如有缺頁或破損，請寄回更換)
有著作權·侵害必究　Printed in Taiwan
ISBN 978-957-32-7892-4
遠流博識網 http://www.ylib.com/
E-mail ylib@ylib.com

國家圖書館出版品預行編目(CIP)資料

快樂就是... : 500個生活裡的小幸福 / 麗莎.史瓦琳(Lisa Swerling)
拉夫.羅拉薩(Ralph Lazar)著；陳思穎譯. -- 初版. -- 臺北市：遠
2016.11
　面；　公分
譯自：Happiness is... : 500 things to be happy about
ISBN 978-957-32-7892-4(平裝)

1.快樂 2.通俗作品

176.51　　　105016794